What's a Virus, Anyway?

The Kids' Book About AIDS

David Fassler, M.D.
Kelly McQueen

Waterfront Books
85 Crescent Road
Burlington, Vermont 05401

Designed and produced by Robinson Book Associates

Printed in the United States

Third printing, July, 1994

Distributed to the book trade by THE TALMAN COMPANY, 150 Fifth Avenue, New York, NY 10011. 1-800-537-8894

Library of Congress Cataloging-in-Publication Data

Fassler, David, et. al.
    What's a virus, anyway?

    Summary: Discusses the deadly disorder known as AIDS.
    1. AIDS (Disease)–Juvenile literature. [1. AIDS (Disease)]
I. McQueen, Kelly, 1962- . II. Title.
RC607.A26F38 1990   89-40719
ISBN 0-914525-15-8 paperback
ISBM 0-914525-14-X plastic comb spiral

Foreword

Like many of you, I find it hard to believe that I really have to talk to my five-year-old daughter and seven-year-old son about a disease as serious as AIDS. Unfortunately, however, AIDS is a fact of life for our children today. The more I learn what young children think about AIDS, and how worried and confused some of them are, the more I understand how important it is for us to teach them about this disease from an early age.

What's a Virus, Anyway? is one of the few books available to help you approach the subject of AIDS with young children. The book explains AIDS in a sensitive manner, using words and concepts children can easily understand. It answers questions honestly and accurately, and encourages children to express their thoughts and concerns. I am sure this book will be an extremely valuable resource for adults and children as they begin to talk together about this difficult topic.

Paula Duncan, M.D.
Coordinator of School Health Services
Burlington, Vermont

Acknowledgements

The preparation of this book was supported, in part, by an educational grant from the Gannett Foundation. We would like to express our appreciation to the *Burlington Free Press* and the Environmental Law Foundation for their help in making this funding possible. We would also like to thank the following friends and colleagues for their encouragement, contributions, and constructive feedback:

Dana Alpern, Ph.D.
Carole Betts, L.Ps.
Lucia Copeland, R.N., M.S.
Sara Copeland
Anna Cotton
Nancy Cotton, Ph.D.
Donna Donovan
Paula Duncan, M.D.
Elise Egeter, M.D.
Anne Epstein, M.D.
Ellen Fassler, M.S.W.
Leonard Fassler
Alan Guttmacher, M.D.

Marcia Hemley, Ph.D.
Donna Jacob
Debby Kelly
Sally Loughridge, Ph.D.
Bruce MacPherson, M.D.
Robert J. McKay, M.D.
Michael McQueen, M.D.
Becky Moore, M.S.W.
Phil Mozeika
Sue Niquette
Mimi Pantuhova, Psy.D.
Carol Phillips, M.D.
Bill Rae, Ph.D.

Frank Reed, Ph.D.
Marc Rucquoi
Amy Rofman
Julie Rofman
Paul Schwartzberg
Sara Simpson
Jennifer Stolz, Ph.D.
Dan Talbert
Kathy Talbert
David Tormey, M.D.
Marty Waldron
Morris Wessel, M.D.

We are also grateful to the many children who shared their thoughts, questions, and creative expressions.

About This Book

AIDS is one of the major health issues facing the world today. Since the disease was first identified in 1981, over 200,000 cases have been diagnosed in the United States alone. It is estimated that the worldwide incidence of AIDS currently exceeds 2,000,000.

AIDS can be a difficult subject to discuss with young children. However, children are already hearing a lot about the disease at a very early age. They hear about AIDS on TV, in school and at home. They talk about AIDS with their friends. Fears and fantasies about AIDS have even entered their playground games.

What's a Virus, Anyway? is designed to help parents and teachers begin to talk about AIDS with young children. The book was written with the help of children between the ages of 5 and 12. It includes their actual drawings and questions, and provides basic information about AIDS in a manner appropriate for this age group.

What's a Virus, Anyway? does not attempt to answer all questions or address all aspects of AIDS. Instead, it is intended to introduce the subject and facilitate further discussion. We hope the book will be a useful tool for parents, teachers and health educators faced with the challenge of explaining AIDS to young children.

David Fassler, M.D.
Kelly McQueen
Burlington, Vermont

A Note About AIDS Education and Sex Education

Understanding the sexual transmission of AIDS is clearly an important component of a comprehensive AIDS education program. Current guidelines recommend addressing the issue of sexual transmission beginning in the sixth grade. We agree that this aspect of the disease need not be overemphasized in educational materials for younger children. We also share the concern that a child's first introduction to information about sex should not be in association with a disease.

What's a Virus, Anyway? is designed to be consistent with current AIDS education curricula for children in grades 1-5. For this reason, the book contains minimal information regarding the sexual transmission of the disease.

We realize that after reading the book, some children may have questions about sex and the sexual transmission of AIDS. Parents, teachers and health educators should respond to such questions honestly and in a manner consistent with the child's existing knowledge and understanding. References on sexuality and sex education are included at the end of the book.

Suggestions for Parents and Teachers

1. Allow children to explore the book at their own pace and in their own manner. Feel free to deviate from the text in response to a child's interests or concerns. The book is intended to stimulate discussion.

2. Answer children's questions honestly, and in a manner appropriate for their developmental level. After offering an answer or explanation, it is helpful to "check back" with the child to see how he or she has understood and incorporated the new information.

3. Don't be afraid to say "I don't know." Tell the child how you will get more information and find answers to questions (e.g., "let's call one of the phone numbers at the back of the book" or "let's write that question down and get the answer the next time we go to the doctor").

4. Learn the facts about AIDS. The more you know, the better you will be able to respond to children's questions. Additional resources about AIDS for parents and teachers are listed at the end of this book.

What's a virus, anyway?

A virus is a tiny, tiny germ. Viruses are like other germs we know about, like bacteria, because they can make people sick. Viruses come in many different shapes and sizes.

Draw a picture of a virus.

VIRUS

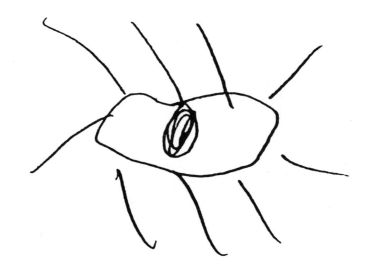

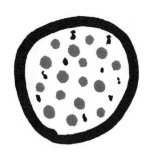

5

How can a virus
Make you sick?

Viruses make you sick by attacking the healthy cells in your body.

Draw a picture of a virus attacking a cell.

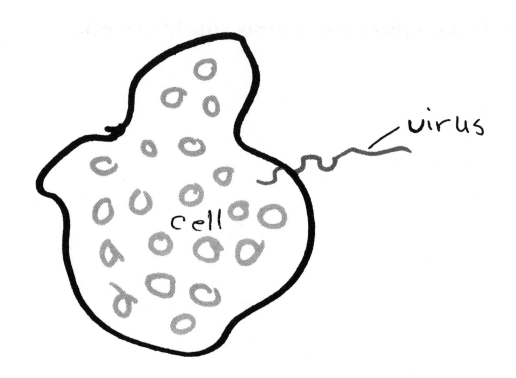

11

The cold virus attacks cells in your nose and throat. That's why you get a cough and a runny nose.

When I had a cough, I had to stay Home From school.

13

There are viruses that attack the cells in your stomach. These viruses can give you a tummy ache.

It's no fun to have a tummy ache.

Some viruses are very common, like the viruses that cause a cold, the flu, and the chicken pox.

the chicken pox

Your body has special cells to help fight viruses that can make you sick. These cells are called *white blood cells*. The white blood cells are important because they help you stay strong and healthy.

Draw a picture of a white blood cell.

20

White cells in a blood vessel

Viruses can be passed from person to person in different ways. Some viruses, like the ones that cause colds and the flu, can be spread by coughing or sneezing. These kinds of viruses are easy to catch.

Some viruses are much harder to catch. Like the virus that causes AIDS.

AiDs? I've heard of that, but I
didn't know that aids was caused

by a virus.

AIDS *is* caused by a virus. The virus is called the HIV.

The HIV is very different from viruses that cause colds and tummy aches. The HIV is hard to catch because it lives in the blood.

The HIV is also more dangerous than most other viruses because it attacks the white blood cells and kills them. When a person doesn't have enough white blood cells, he or she can become very sick and get what we call AIDS.

What is AiDs, anyway?

AIDS stands for:

Acquired

Immune

Deficiency

Syndrome

Acquired means that the disease was caught after the person was exposed to the virus.

Immune **D**eficiency means that the person doesn't have enough white blood cells to fight off infections.

We call it a **S**yndrome because a person who has AIDS has a lot of different sick feelings and symptoms.

How does someone get AiDs?

People get AIDS from other people who have the HIV in their blood.

People who take drugs can get AIDS by using the same needles.

A man or a woman can get AIDS by having sex with a person who has the HIV in his or her blood.

Babies can get AIDS even before they're born if their moms have AIDS.

You *can't* get AIDS from:

- mosquito bites

- toilet seats

- drinking fountains

- touching or hugging

- shots or needles at the doctor's

- coughing and sneezing

- sharing food or toys

You can't get aids From a Mosquito

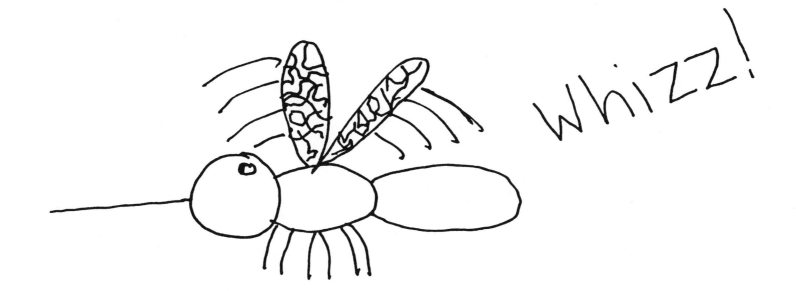

Whizz!

Who does get aids?

There's no one kind of person who gets AIDS. There are young people and old people, boys and girls, and people from different countries who have AIDS.

Draw a picture of a person with AIDS.

A Man With AIDS.
He's getting Skinny.

40

A baby with aiDs

People With AiDS are Just like every body else.

A person With aids feeling
Happy

A person With Aids feeling
Sad

A person With Aids feeling Sick

A boy with Aids Skiing with his Friends.

What happens to people
With Aids?

Some people with AIDS can live for a few years or even longer. Others get very sick and die in just a short time.

A person With Aids

Before

After

at First

Later

53

Will they ever
Find a cure
for
Aids ?

Scientists and doctors are working very hard to find a cure for AIDS. They *have* found medicines that can help some people with AIDS live longer and feel better, but we still don't have a cure.

Sometimes I Worry
about AIDS.

What should I do?

If you feel scared or worried about AIDS, you can talk to your parents and teachers, your doctor, or the school nurse. They can answer your questions and help you understand more about AIDS.

It's important to learn about AIDS by asking lots of questions.

What are your questions about AIDS?

These pages are for you to make up stories or poems or draw any pictures you want.

Resources

Agencies and Organizations

National AIDS Hotline
Centers for Disease Control
800-342-AIDS (English)
800-344-SIDA (Spanish)
800-AIDS-TTY (TTY/TDD)

AIDS Action Committee
131 Clarendon Street
Boston, MA 02116
617-437-6200
617-536-7733 (Hotline)

National AIDS Information
   Clearinghouse
PO Box 6003
Rockville, MD 20850
800-458-5231

American Academy of Child
   and Adolescent Psychiatry
Committee on HIV Issues
3615 Wisconsin Ave., N.W.
Washington, DC 20016
202-966-7300

American Foundation
   for AIDS Research
1515 Broadway, Suite 3601
New York, NY 10036
212-719-0033

American Red Cross
AIDS Education Office
1709 New York Ave. N.W.
Washington, DC 20006
202-434-4074

Health Education Resource
   Organization (HERO)
101 West Read Street
Suite 812
Baltimore, MD 21201
301-685-1180

San Francisco AIDS
   Foundation
P.O. Box 6182
San Francisco, CA 94101
415-861-3397

The AIDS Health Project
Box 0884
San Francisco, CA 94143
415-476-6430

AIDS Resource Center
National PTA
700 North Rush Street
Chicago, IL 60611
312-787-0977

Pediatric AIDS Network
Children's Hospital
   of Los Angeles
4650 Sunset Boulevard, Box 55
Los Angeles, CA 90027
213-669-5616

AID Atlanta
1132 W. Peachtree Street, NW
Suite 102
Atlanta, GA 30309
800-342-2437

Pan American Health
  Organization/WHO
AIDS Program
525 23rd Street, N.W.
Washington, D.C. 20037
202-861-4346

Association for the Care
  of Children's Health
3615 Wisconsin Avenue, N.W.
Washington, DC 20016
301-654-6549

March of Dimes
Birth Defect Foundation
1275 Mamaroneck Avenue
White Plains, NY 10805
914-428-7100

American Academy
  of Pediatrics
Committee on School Health
141 NW Point Boulevard
P.O. Box 297
Elk Grove Village, IL 60009-0927
800-433-9016

Canadian Agencies and Organizations:

National AIDS Hotline
  of Canada
800-267-7712 (English)
800-668-AIDS (English)
800-267-FIDA (French)

AIDS Committee Toronto
  (ACT)
P.O. Box 55, Station F
Toronto, Ontario M4Y 2L4
416-926-1626 (Hotline)

Montreal Health Press
CP1000,
Station Place Du Parc
Montreal, Quebec H2W 2N1
514-282-1171

Comité FIDA de Montreal
3600 Hotel de Ville Ave
Montreal, Quebec H2X 3V6
514-282-9888

Canadian AIDS Society
267 Dalhousie Street #201
Ottawa, Ontario K1N 7E3
613-238-5014
613-238-4111 (Hotline)

64

References

Books for Parents and Teachers

About AIDS:

Alyson, S. (ed.). *You Can Do Something About AIDS.* Boston: Stop AIDS Project and Company, 1988.

American Responds to AIDS. *AIDS Prevention Guide for Parents and Other Adults Concerned About Youth.* Washington, DC: Centers for Disease Control, 1989.

Quackenbush, M., and Villarreal, S. *Does AIDS Hurt?* Santa Cruz, CA: Network Publications, 1988.

Ralston, A. *What Do Our Children Need to Know About AIDS? Guidelines for Parents.* Novato, CA: Beneficial Publishing, 1988.

About Sexuality and Sex Education:

Calderone, M. and Ramey, J. *Talking With Your Child About Sex: Questions and Answers for Children from Birth to Puberty.* New York: Ballentine Books, 1982.

Gitchel, S. and Foster, L. *Let's Talk About... S-E-X.* Fresno, CA: Planned Parenthood of Central California, 1987.

Planned Parenthood Federation of America. *How to Talk With Your Child About Sexuality.* Garden City, New York: Doubleday and Company, 1986.

Ratner, M. and Chamlin, S. *Straight Talk.* New York: Penguin, 1987.

Books for Elementary School Children

Hausherr, R. *Children and the AIDS Virus.* New York: Clarion Books, 1989.

Hyde, M., and Forsyth, E. *Know About AIDS.* New York: Walker and Company, 1987.

Lerner, E. *Understanding AIDS.* Minneapolis: Lerner, 1987.

Books for Adolescents

Warren, C. *Understanding and Preventing AIDS*. Chicago: Children's Press, 1988.

Silverstein, A., and Silverstein, V. *AIDS: Deadly Threat*. Hillside, N.J.: Enslow, 1986.

de Saint Phalle, N. *AIDS: You Can't Catch It Holding Hands*. San Francisco: 1987.

Hyde, M., and Forsyth, E. *AIDS: What Does It Mean to You?* New York: Walker and Company, 1987.

About the Authors

David Fassler, M.D. is a child psychiatrist practicing in Burlington, Vermont. A graduate of the Yale University School of Medicine, Dr. Fassler received his training in adult psychiatry at the University of Vermont, and in child psychiatry at the Cambridge Hospital, Harvard Medical School. He is currently a clinical assistant professor and the director of continuing education in the Department of Psychiatry at the University of Vermont, and an instructor in psychiatry at Cambridge Hospital. Dr. Fassler is also a co-author of a series of children's books dealing with family transitions.

Kelly McQueen is a medical student at the University of Vermont. She received her undergraduate training in biology at Colorado College. Ms. McQueen has coordinated an extensive research effort on children's perceptions of AIDS. She has also coordinated the production of an educational videotape about AIDS for young children.

WHAT'S A VIRUS, ANYWAY?
The Kids' Book About AIDS
David Fassler, M.D. & Kelly McQueen

AIDS can be a difficult subject to discuss with young children. However, children hear a lot about the disease at a very early age. *What's a Virus, Anyway?* is a simple introduction to help adults talk with children. It provides basic information in a manner appropriate for 4-10 year olds.

"… that people with AIDS are just like everyone else makes this book particularly distinctive." — *Booklist*

Also, now a new Spanish edition:
¿QUE ES UN VIRUS?
Un Libro Para Niños Sobre el SIDA

$8.95 paper, $12.95 plastic comb spiral
Ages 4-10. 70 pages. Illustrated by children

THE DIVORCE WORKBOOK
A Guide for Kids and Families
Sally B. Ives, Ph.D., David Fassler, M.D.,
and Michelle Lash, M.Ed., A.T.R.

The volume takes children by the hand from marriage through separation, divorce and 'legal stuff' which defines such terms as custody, child support, divorce mediation, and visitation. It also devotes considerable attention to the emotional aftermath of divorce."

— **Nadine Brozan**, *New York Times*

$12.95 paper, $16.95 plastic comb spiral,
160 pages, illustrated by children. Ages 4-12

CHANGING FAMILIES
A Guide for Kids and Grown-ups
David Fassler, M.D., Michelle Lash, M.Ed., A.T.R.
and Sally B. Ives, Ph.D.

This book helps children cope with the emotional confusion of being in a changing family. Divorce, remarriage, new surroundings, and new relatives are a few of the changes presented for discussion here.

"Many children of divorce openly or secretly hope that their biological parents will reunite. The new marriage shatters that illusion." —**David Fassler**, *during interview with Lawrence Kutner, in "Parent & Child," New York Times*

$14.95 paper, $18.95 plastic comb spiral
192 pages, illustrated by children. Ages 4-12

COMING TO AMERICA
The Kids' Book about Immigration
David Fassler, M.D. and Kimberly Danforth, M.A.

Many refugee children have experienced war, desperate circumstances, or natural disasters. Written and drawn with the help of children between the ages of 5 and 12, *Coming to America* can facilitate open and honest discussion about a child's immigration experience.

"It has a genuine voice which children and families will find comforting."
—**Caroline Linse**, *Ministry of Education, Riga, Latvia*

$12.95 paper, $16.95 plastic comb spiral
160 pages, illustrated by children. Ages 5-12

"MY DAD'S *Definitely* NOT A DRUNK!"
Elisa Lynn Carbone

A realistic and sensitive portrayal of family dynamics in an alcoholic's home…. Few books for this age group effectively convey the experiences of children in this situation without villainizing the parent. Carbone not only does the job nicely, but also provides good information in the process."
—*School Library Journal, Fall 1992*

$7.95 paper, $11.95 hardcover
100 pages. Grades 6-9.

WATERFRONT BOOKS
85 Crescent Road, Burlington, VT 05401
Order toll-free: 1-800-639-6063

MY KIND OF FAMILY
A Book for Kids in Single-Parent Homes
Michelle Lash, M.Ed., Sally Ives Loughridge, Ph.D.,
and David Fassler, M.D.

Helps children express, explore and understand some of the special issues and feelings associated with living in a single-parent home.

$14.95 paper, $18.95 plastic comb spiral
208 pages, illustrated by children. Ages 4-12

JOSH
A Boy with Dyslexia
Caroline Janover

An adventure story for kids with a section of resources and facts about learning disabilities.

*"In **Josh**, Caroline Janover has taken me into the mind and heart of **A Boy with Dyslexia**. We share his fears, tragedies, and triumphs. Must reading for all families who struggle with dyslexia."*
—**Mary MacCracken**, *educational therapist and author of **Lovey, Turnabout Children**, and **Circle of Children***

$7.95 paper, $11.95 hardcover
100 pages, 15 illustrations. Ages 8-12

LUKE HAS ASTHMA, TOO
Alison Rogers
Illustrated by Michael Middleton

The story shows that asthma can be managed in a calm fashion. For the more than two million families who have children with asthma, this is an important message." — **Thomas F. Plaut, M.D.,** *author of **Children with Asthma: A Manual for Parents***

$6.95 paper
32 pages, illustrated. Ages 3-7

LET'S TALK TRASH
The Kids' Book About Recycling
Kelly McQueen and David Fassler, M.D.

Never has 'talking trash' been so much fun! This book takes a refreshing look at a tough problem. I hope kids will share this book with their parents so that we all understand why it's important to protect our beautiful environment."
—**Madeleine M. Kunin**, *Governor of Vermont*

$14.95 paper, $18.95 plastic comb spiral
168 pages, illustrated by children. Ages 4-10